I0086596

Crackers in Bed

Crackers in Bed

A Second Collection of Poetry

by

Lynda G. Bullerwell

Crackers in Bed
Copyright © 2015 Lynda G. Bullerwell
All Rights Reserved

No part of this publication may be reproduced, stored in a retrieval system or transmitted in any form or by any means, electronic, mechanical, photocopying, recording or otherwise, without the prior written permission of both the copyright owner and the publisher of this book.

ISBN-13: 978-0692375334
ISBN-10: 0692375333

Published by Water Forest Press
PO Box 295, Stormville, NY 12582
WaterForestPress.com

Layout & Design by V.R. Valentine
Edited by P. Valentine

Cover Art © by Billy Mathis
http://www.themathisstudio.com/
Lynda's back cover photo by Tim Bullerwell

This is a work of fiction. Any similarities to real people living or deceased are purely coincidental. Events, locales and characters in this book have been composed into fictional form, unless otherwise stated in interviews & articles by the author. All material herein is the property and responsibility of the author.

To my children and grandchildren who bring me joy,
my mom, sister, and in-laws who bring encouragement,
friends and poets who bring me inspiration,
God and my angels who bring me hope

And last, but not least,
my husband, Tim who brings me laughter, love, light...
and crackers in bed.

Lynda G. Bullerwell

Acknowledgments

I would like to thank the following publications in which some of the following poems have appeared:

The Cherry Muse
Epiphany Magazine
The River Muse
Miracle e-zine

Thanks to Billy Mathis photographer for Mathis Studios for creating the cover photo.
http://www.themathisstudio.com/

"Let me live, love, and say it well in good sentences"

~ Sylvia Plath

Poems

Poems

Envy of a Muse

I always wanted to be envied
for syllables I whisper;
bring anticipation

of my next line

like the poets I have loved
that never loved me back,

but, maybe this dream we live
is enough;
this sparkle that never leaves
when sleepy heads fall upon pillows
and goodnight kisses

last until morning.

This muse, she awakens me
with an ache that won't subside

until heads turn,
two hold hands and whisper
to the rhythm of words

I thought went unnoticed.

I would strum chords;
dance my way into your heart
making sure the smile

never fades,

paint blooms on every flower
your eyes gaze upon
drying teardrops

as we share my sun,

because, for a poet,
it is never enough.

Flowers at Sylvia&s Feet (for Sylvia Plath)

Perhaps
you were meant to bloom
only for a season,
kiss us with syllables
pulling heartstrings
to dance,

then flutter away,

like April does
when the flowers
have blossomed.

Perhaps
your milk and honey skin
was too pure for this wind;
too fragile for winter

when the green is gone.

Oh, Sylvia,
you try to pull us down with you
to lie in your words
like the flowers,

you left.

Blowing Out the Candles

One more year and I am still waiting;

checking the mailbox for a card
(even though I know you don't have my address,)
and the phone for missed calls,

hoping for some storybook reunion.

How many letters marked "return to sender"
must one receive before the dark realization
strikes a cord

in the head of this dreamy-eyed
fatherless fool?

I can take the candles from the cake,
one   by   one
and count the memories

without you in them,
wash dishes so tears
turn to soap scum
before anyone notices
the faded smile

and close thoughts away in the cupboard
as if nothing ever happened.

Her

I want to write *that* classic;
the one people remember;
the one that leaves you different

than when you came,

profound, like Plath;
melting your heart in a puddle,
like Neruda.
I want to be beautiful, like Elizabeth,
with the darkness of Poe
and the light of Emily.

I want to paint gardens with syllables
and warm skies to sunrise;

Frost,
staying golden
when the rest of the world
is monotone.

I want quotation marks on my tombstone,
tears upon pink roses
for her,
you know,

the one who wrote *that* poem.

No Vacancy

It's the emptiness
in the pit of your stomach,
the cry in a street singer's guitar
when passersby toss a quarter
in a worn out black hat

and the street lamps fade
as the taxicab waits
for the last customer of the night
stumbling in stilettos;
lights flashing at the intersection
of pomp and circumstance
where a man sells white roses,
a single or a dozen,

and a no vacancy sign
is the only thing anyone will remember

in the morning.

Ghost Town

Music opens that weak wound and I take three steps behind
pulse pulling me further back to dark corners, corneas
retracting light like fireflies between faith and a broken moon.
I felt the whisper of something wilted begging for life
in that sandwich shop in Jefferson;
      red memories on stairwells
and sad rain even on Saturday evening
      gatherings, downtown
when song takes pain from tattered souls leaving new breath
making misers into kings with only a touch of laughter
and a few scattered chords to linger on until mourning.
Take the slow train to reality because there is no colder place
than one where you cannot dream letters into sand
      and share words
with strangers, throwing leftover syllables over the bridge
for lovers to find and fawn over
      when stars are full of sky and eyes
glisten upon rippling waters wrestling waves
      for moon's full attention.
Never let the tremble make it to an ache
      while your lashes still flutter
and his lips are calling, and close enough to touch with yours.

Daughters

With tiny cries and outstretched fists
you peeked through dew kissed lashes
into my new found, fluttering heart

with coos that whispered to be cuddled;
soft breaths that murmured gratitude.

cherishing every smile,
I kissed every tiny finger
and as you slept, I prayed,

giving praise for every new awakening.

Such a joy, these flowers
springing from loving earth;
these once wobbly, stemmed buds
blossoming into graceful, dancing
petaled visions of beauty;

these daughters of mine.

Limp

I remember the way you hung your head;
complexion, white with panic, limbs
shaking, lyrics pause when rebuttal failed,
and after all of the accusations, it was you
sowing seeds in another garden, heavy sun
shedding light on actuality, pride aching,
every inch of me held together with nothing
but echoes; clouds of incessant reverberation.
Bells chime softer now that I know love
even in winter when snowdrops fall, limp
but, never, never as weak as you.

On a Night Without Stars

There is so much more to love
than anyone could ever conceive of.

Hands, reaching out to help you up
when you think you cannot take
one   more   step,

arms that find their way
around a fractured mess of a girl
once smiling, now sobbing thing
curled up in a conundrum,
stoop, and pick up the pieces,
(never complaining,)

of something he never broke.

Ears that have listened
to the same sad story, time after time
knowing there will be
the same nagging {three letter question}
in the end

and nothing to say

to stitch up a shredded heart
left by someone with only a gene
and a name ~
in common.

A voice
with a whisper
louder to the spirit than any sound,

but God.

A smile that illuminates
every inch of her sky
on a night without any stars,

and those eyes,

those eyes that even without words
can make all of the ugliness disappear

until the next time.

Ivory (and All the Colors In Between)

As fingers tickled piano keys,
I felt the plucking of each string
in unison:

tender amidst raging riffs
soft, then heavy
like syllables, adjoined

in the perfect sentence.

I see his face, tranquil
eyes closed, head back;
passionate within chords

as if just being born
into someone else's symphony.

From Pablo to Plath

The contrast between life and you
has me reeling; intoxicated
on possibilities, torn between dreams
and the images that lurk in corners
of a once darkened dwelling.

Your pink roses make me smile,

but, here I am crying to a song
in a music box

over things that aren't fair,
people that aren't here,
wondering just what forces

allowed me *to be.*

I don't believe poets string syllables
into pitch perfect assonance
only when their hearts are broken;

strumming chords on harp strings

unpredictably jumping
from Pablo to Plath.

Poetic Transfusion

I.
Some of us are born in love
with words and how syllables
play on the tongue and lips
like sweet challenges
for the soul to dabble in.
I will waltz with alliteration,
never stepping on a dance floor
and paint intricate flowers,
tracing every petal; fingertips
never touching a brush.

II.
Look in the sky. What do you see?
I gaze upon a million constellations-
clandestine sparks of inspiration.
I see love, life, death, pain;
a thousand moments glimmering
before my eyes. I see the miracle
that we all share the same blue,
clouded, big beautiful sky
even if I have never met you,
seen your lips, curved like the moon.
I can imagine you, dream you,
create you with a stroke of my pen.

III.
Some say I speak too much of love.
I may say his whisper at night
before the lights go out, makes me melt,
or mention the scent of his cologne that lingers
long after the goodbye kiss in the morning.
I may reminisce of his proposal on one knee
or quote lines from his sonnets
that I fell in love with before we met.
You can have too much sleep,
weight, soda, carbs, rain, heat, snow,
darkness, pain, negativity, make-up,
but, you can never, ever
have too much love, or poetry,
for, they are one in the same,
and as vital as oxygen
or the beating of this heart.

Shaking the Stars

If we could shake the stars
and bring the moon to its knees
to see just one sun,
blow out the darkness
from hollow, seeping clouds,
we could just find a soft place
to fall.

That one flower growing petals
in tainted soil, through a crack
in cement expectations
where children hop scotch
tossing pebbles,
counting steps
until that one leap of faith.

She takes it with wings
feathered, flying
barefoot dreamy-eyed fate
painted from spring hue
calm cascading through silk strands
tickling ivory in symmetry
of dancing thoughts,

and here she thought syllables
were wasted
in journals
of glass slipper reunions;
endings, happy, but distant
like dandelions blown south,

and then here he came
windswept, white horse drawn
lover, loving her, this unchanged,
unchained flower child
kissed by the mere existence
of such fondness, this feeling
like lightning
without a chance of rain.

Lynda G. Bullerwell

Hiding Behind a Muse

I'll just let her take the pen
and drive thoughts home
while I sit in the passenger seat;

a reader,

enjoying the fruits muse can produce
in a perfect growing season.

I could plant seeds
Into perfect little rows
praying for rain to kiss petals
and blossom the finest words
a sun can punctuate.

I can speak in third person,
giggle at myself and smile
at just the right moment
so no one will notice it is her
who is twirling ink, spinning feather,
spilling alliteration mixed with tears

from a heart that has waited years
to beat in this red rhythm,

or I could hide here behind my muse
fluttering out syllables gently
until that big crescendo
because I can pour my soul out
until I make the whole world cry

and it still wouldn't be good enough

for you.

Ticking

The clock is always ticking,
ticking somewhere
and I keep running
on someone else's watch.

That telephone, just sitting there;
the elephant in the room
toying with my emotions

and the ticking never stops

I can see them; hear them in my sleep
like chapters, forming;

the single mother, waitressing
while latch key kids grow up too fast
on frozen dinners
and one sided conversations
with animated companions

as the guy holding a cardboard sign
in the corner of Eastchase and Interstate 30
swallows his pride
while people avoid making eye contact
with their worst fears exemplified.

There is a young executive
climbing the corporate ladder
long nights, lonely weekends
at the keyboard;
her biological clock ticking-
visions swirling in her coffee cup

and the ticking never stops
as these syllables play in my dreams,
lining up in stanzas

just waiting to become a poem.

After New Year's Eve

They took away her flowers
from the corner
where the light blinks red, now.

They never fixed that traffic light
after New Year's eve.

I still remember her

and picture it in my mind;
laughter, speed
screams, then silence
just after the fireworks, toasts,
kisses at midnight;
confetti flying like the glass
across the intersection

between life and death.

I wondered who laid those pastel flowers
delicately upon the grass
letting them get drier each time.

They took away her flowers,
but, I still see her blooming.

Embracing the Gray

Field of dandelions beckons
in whispers
from unfamiliar places

as every flutter finds something new
to fall in love with.

When lashes close, make a wish

and blow,

or wait for constellations
and watch the world
from the ground up;

fireflies in perfect symmetry
with the glimmer in a lover's gaze.

Even in Winter,
passion blooms tenderness
upon petal-less flowers

on afternoons shaded gray.

Fabrication of You

Accusations run rampant
between white sheep
in glass houses

while pleas of love are fruitless
like those ladders you climb

leading nowhere but the top

where you find nothing
but pats on the back
from nameless faces

and a mirror
that you are forced to look into.

Attic Treasures

Flickers of light
beg to slip through cracks;
tiny footsteps
on wood floors, creak.

Grandma had an attic.
There were cobwebs
the smell of books,
my Mom's old roller skates
and the doll with button eyes
I thought I had lost.

There were stacks of reader's digests
and there was a hiding place
where tears were allowed
(even for little girls);

the only place I could breathe
and let dreams out to play;
just me and my pen

scribbling secrets in a big chief tablet.

A Novel Idea

I will never apologize
for alliteration
or stop breathing

after syllables

reveling
for your attention.

You can word count
in November
and chalk up chapters
one through five
as beginnings of new best seller,

and I will concentrate
on the beauty of constellations

in April,

and twenty words that bring you
out of the darkness
and to your knees,

if it takes me fifty tries
to woo your senses.

There is something beautiful
about an unfinished poem
swirling in my sleep,
churning thoughts like butter

more delectable with age.

Pass me another dollop
of inspiration,
and I will fill your plate
with a dish sweeter
than a craving,

something more savory
than any adjective

ever whispered from your lips.

Lynda G. Bullerwell

Chromatic Chords From a Beat Up Fender

I turned the corner
to see where that sun beam
was shining;
guitar case lying open
passers by pitched quarters
while I stood, star struck
by this voice,
this voice
that seemed to fall from the heavens
like some lost star, reunited;

this unshaven smiling vision
of what the world has come to.

He sang about peace
as his guitar cried
over what his eyes had seen.

Someone handed him a drink
and asked about the medals
that adorned his faded denim jacket.
He said: "I fought for my country
and lived to tell it."

Every line in his face
retold that story;
his mind
tuning out insufferable sounds

with chromatic chords
to soothe a haunted soul.

Cocktail Hour

Why do starless nights seem so heavy
dragging out every metaphor
kicking and screaming
before moonlight can take hold
and be the gravity
in a room of imbalance?

These curtains do nothing
to hold out the darkness

when past keeps peeking through
slipping in slurs
that no one wants to hear about.

If you are in love,
you're not supposed to talk about it
or let lips bring comfort to a gray hour
when the six-o-clock news drowns dreams
turning soft clouds into torrents
that pound sense into anything forgiving.

One shot from the past makes ripples
in your toast to hope,
and faith falters and falls to the bottom
of your glass

bringing a worn out lament
to its final crescendo.

We Could Love (for Maya Angelou)

If time should stand still
just long enough for us to touch;
to breathe the same whispered air,
you would love me.

If memories were butterflies
within our shared grasp
you could see my struggles, and I yours,
hold hands with possibilities
and drown all bitter thoughts
in a sea of no regrets.

A kiss on the cheek could mean the end
of battle, of hate,
of everything that made you think less
of another.

Just think,
if Earth could shake loose in orbit
spin off of its conditioned axis
and land on neutral ground,

we could mingle in new light
void of colors; of prejudice in any form
creating a downpour of kindness

and we could just love.

Wet Paint

The ink won't dry
in the spaces between you

and I.

We are syllables
connected by more than breaths
and borrowed adjectives.

There is something about whispers
under the covers
anticipating traces of fingertips
upon waiting curves

that makes me miss you more.

If words could paint my love
upon a canvas,
mine would be a masterpiece
and the world would see
naked truth;

not colored or cliché
hiding behind eyes

that may have never seen light.

Gypsy Mama

She is art wrapped in poetry
strands of fabric colored orange;
daisies in her hair

as blue eyes speak peace
from the back of the bus

unafraid to defend things unjust.

I danced in chords
from her generation;
a hippy born too late,
never fitting in

or standing out;

just a quiet image
with words to spill
in ink, read and flowing

like the bond, strong
between a Mother

and her child.

Speaking in Daffodil Tongue

I hear you echo now

as leaves fall
and red birds
seem much more distant.

You could have stayed
until dawn broke us both
and light upon petals
no longer made me melt.

Will you have time for me
when rivers flow slower
and stars seem less brilliant
in the mist of so much heaven?

I never longed for chill;
blankets covering
nature's precious prairie muse.

I am still speaking in daffodil tongue
skipping in syllables

that grow in sun.

Hearts grow fonder
when white trains drag earth
through Saturdays in June;
winds carrying shared love
from tossed tresses
of a runaway bride's bouquet.

I still remember that first picnic
writing poetry;
kissing
between stanzas
behind that old oak tree.

There just aren't enough adjectives
to make me love winter more.

The Fabric of Life

Oh, those stars I dreamt on
peeking through the clothesline
searching for solace between sheets

pinned up with regret

stiff, like muscles that held me upright
when I wanted to fall down
with those autumn leaves,
when gold,
seemed dreary as rust
through misty eyes.

Who were you to drain light
leaving my slivers of faith
to fill the void;
wounded promise of love
seeping through the cracks.

I could only imagine the sound of leaves
predicting winter,
lashes aching for flakes of snow
to awaken senses

and, oh, those flowers
blooming in spring,
windswept wing song,

softness of petal
raging strength from timid clouds
rising like sea foam,
secrets, to the surface.

Afflictions,
you have yours and I have mine.
I rumble, volcanic ramblings
in ink, clamoring for attention
like lightening, thunder;

symmetry in an intimate setting.

Oh, why can't I paint you away
now that I hold the brush,
and you, yes you, are the canvas;
cracked, faded, broken
like my heart was
every time you stung
with words, sharper than swords

shredding anything left
of me.

At Twenty Seven

There is light behind these eyes
and rivers flowing between mountains
bare feet have tread upon

when valleys were deeper
than the worries that traveled them.

There are scars, unseen
behind precious little lies;
feet of crows remaining
after smiles fade
and whispers become the voice
that roared when starlight shone
upon falling wishes
of some restless romantic.

Too many moons
have made way for suns
rising like legends
that fell at twenty seven

never seeing past the blur;
the power one hungers for
until the lights go down

and things are not so pretty,
anymore.

Slipping Through the Cracks

I threw a dollar in the hat
but it was so much more
than that.

There was heart;

There was blues slipping through
every sidewalk crack,
beautiful chords flowing
from worn out sneakers

and fingers

worn to the bone,
still strumming
to a chorus

only old souls can hear.

No Room for April Flowers

You left in Spring,
my favorite season
when love
and everything with petals,

blooms.

You said you would be here
on birdsong mornings
for coffee
and conversations I could only have
with you.

I couldn't listen to Elvis
because every strum stroked that place
where pain meets pulse and promises
of porch swings on Sundays

took a back seat to fate.

I feel you in the wind and see
all these fluttering things
you appear to me in;
all with wings,

and I know why.

I left part of my soul in those forget-me-nots
that I can never get back;
syllables resting, floating in rivers
of too many words left unsaid.

Thank you for Autumn's crunch
and the tickle of snowflakes,
(rare for a Texas Christmas eve),

but, March will never rain the same
without your hands
holding my white roses.

They tore out the bush you planted
and left me

with this hole in my heart.

Red

I.

Poppies in any other month
wouldn't be so crucial
as dead weight,
floating air;
past participles, glistened
on paper, bled,
bleached white,
words so invisible,

II.

no one
can see the dark,
the cold of pupils void of light.
You paint me rosy,
deep red when you're angry,
but I am nothing but blue
when stars gleam sapphire,
saffron imagination weeping
ripples wafting this love
to modest meadows for miles
of nothing but blushing sky.

III.

In January, when gray steals sun
and pansies lie in waiting
for delicate tumbling weeds
to dance in, dreamy eyed;

copper mornings- wishes
hanging on clothes lines
like strings of hearts
every Valentine's day.

IV.

Hear those church bells
chime like there is no tomorrow
while dusty autobiographies
tell tender stories over coffee
to anyone who will listen
and here I am yearning
for just one more barefoot stroll
and four initials in wet sand.

V.

We will get to San Josef again-
take another unpaved road,
all uphill
and watch poppies flicker,
from a distance,
like Sylvia did, bleeding red,
and hot as July.

Lynda G. Bullerwell

Unconditional

You returned my heart today-
not in the pretty package
in which you received it,

but tattered, broken
and missing a piece.

I thought I understood love;
unconditional, untarnished,
but, you showed me new colors
in rust, ruffled,
weathered, beaten brown

like a lost kitten
limping back home.

Cry of Autumn

Willows weeping,
changing colors,
silent and swaying
like harps stroked
by flowing fingers of love.

We all are suspect
to the mood of wind
and only those with wings
can bring sun

to branches with the will
to grow.

Wrap every last twig
with seeds to flower
as clouds spill life

upon unsuspecting buds.

Sunday&'s Child

I.

My January gift, wrinkled,
ruffled, wrapped in blue
sweet solemn little bundle, quiet.
Pale, like me, predictable as stars.

I didn't know why you never cried
or why your eyes wouldn't meet mine,

but, I sang to you anyway.

II.

At three,

they used medical terms to label you,
told me all the things you would never do.
To them, you were a diagnosis
in a medical book. a statistic,
another autistic child in the system.

but, to me, you were my heart,
my beautiful raven haired boy.

III.

Tomorrow

is your thirty-fourth birthday.
You still brighten my day
with just a smile

and you don't need words
to say I love you
when that look in your eyes
is a novel in the making,
a celebration of life,
from an innocent's perspective.
This may not be poetic,
but, you are;

my angel boy,
my January gift.

Under the Bridge

Why would one miss days
of smoldering moments
turn to ashes

or smothering seconds;
time crawling like spiders
into a web you spun
to keep an innocent victim

hostage.

No, abuse is not only a fist,
or a slap

like you wanted me to believe.
It was words that burned,
degrading syllables that stung
as psalms sang
in my head to keep me sane.

It was darkness
when my soul was hungry
for light.

There is a bond stronger
than the chains;
rays that seep through walls;
a love, unconditional
to pierce the gray,

to save a heart
from a poisoned fate.
There is a calm, now,

after the storm.

Metaphor Envy

Pen your heart away
as I look on, admiringly
envious of your metaphor,

my syllables, intimidated
by your presence,
usual phrases, feeling redundant,
borrowing crumbs
to feed my muse.

Swept off my feet
by your lack of concern
for "proper" punctuation

never allowing emotion
to get lost in the shuffle

of elements;
a downpour of pulsating vowels
and consonants;

your words sashaying around

like there are no rules
in poetry.

When Star Dust Settles

Weeping willows shelter weak hearts;
cardinals singing love songs
to unsuspecting *flowers*,

flowers dance to wind songs
softer than his whispers were
on my cheek that first *summer*.

Summer comes and goes like fireflies
when the moon hides
like tiny ballerinas *tiptoeing*

Tiptoeing over hearts that bleed
sorrows into syllables;
words understood only by *poets*.

Poets collect adjectives in shoeboxes
like treasures for tomorrow
when rocking chairs no longer collect *dust.*

Dust settles from stars, enamored
as perfect pictures never develop,
but, comfort does, settling like *quiet*

Quiet mornings with only eyes
fluttering conversation, filling with tears
like weeping willows do.

Epidemic

You slipped past my instincts
with convincing conversation
to soothe vulnerability

masking your own tendencies,
temporarily

like home remedies
for the common cold.

Blindsided,
I watched my insecurities grow
like weeds beneath my feet

as little pieces of me faded

like the little girl
who caught snowflakes on her tongue.

Fairy tales
became my reality

for someday.

Now, the glass slipper fits
and light fills my castle
as his breaths of whisper
bring sighs to my sanctuary.

Try as you may,
you cannot infect love
with hate.

I just wish there was some wonder drug
that could cure the symptoms

of you.

Barefoot Love

As April bids us adieu,
her moist kisses painting petals
to dance upon,

we stammer in verse
to articulate the beauty
of such a delicate season.
Skies rise and set;

mortals like us
taking terra cotta steps;
swirling skirts brushing over daffodils

barefoot love upon blades of grass

as luster sashays through gardens
like the goddess of Spring.

Daddy&s Little Girl

You held baby hands that first April,
felt that soft coo upon your cheek,
looked into the same blue-green eyes
that haunt you now, tear filled, unworthy,
(or so you tell yourself) on those late nights
when thoughts try to escape a thin skinned,
well dressed, businessman mindset
you created to mask the reflection
in the mirror asking why on mornings
when rain isn't the only thing carried in
on those shiny leather shoes; muddy
visions of roles we play like parts
in some overrated after school movie.
I am stronger without that pat on the head,
kiss on the cheek, grins on prom night
kind of mentality, and who needs a Father
to tell a girl she is beautiful. After all,
that whole "daddy's little girl "thing
has always been a little overrated,
or that is what I keep telling myself.

Quiet Lucidity

Pour me from petals
soft breath, still heart
commiserating with demons;

smoke rings swirling

over late night coffee
and conversation.

I can hear the jingles from here;
a scant recollection
of past pretense,

but tonight is full of stars;
your eyes reflecting so much more
than ribbons and bows.

There is something holy
about trust, kindness
and the quiet peace
of wrapped silhouettes
showering our sky

love, covered in moonbeams
with a different way of light,

moving,
shifting normalcy;
this luminous starlight
lending lucidity
to a half-beaten culture

that just needs a miracle
to believe in.

Asking Apparitions to Dance

Clouds gather to mourn
amidst monuments,
stone memories
and embedded tears;

pitter patter of hoofs
and heartbreak
sound echoes

through the elements.

Flowing tresses, tamed
as figures immortalized under stars
and bending moon cries spill

upon cement fabrications

of daring.
Dancers swirl in colors
like rainbows
asking apparitions to dance;
one angel, exalted
in the center of souls

asking passers-by to reminisce
finding comfort in being the scenery;
the chosen one, left behind

keeping heroes
and their history

alive

the Price of Freedom

I came to you leafless;
windblown tresses swaying;
a starry-eyed dreamer
plucking petals

from a borrowed wildflower bouquet.

How can one venture to take
something as fragile as a heart,
still beating to the chords of conviction,

and silence the strumming
of love's most tender verse?

You left me in the rain;
peeled back, hollow
with nothing but a notebook of thoughts
the clothes on my back,
and the faith that Grandma gave me.

It turns out that was all I needed

to be free.

Stumbling

Lines on these blank pages start becoming blurry
when you search for perfect syllables;
that imminent ending in perfect alliteration
found at the bottom of that last cup of coffee,
now cold.

He promised to keep the bed warm
while I empty thoughts from a haunted pillow
overstuffed with unmarried words wrestling to escape
through these fingertips, frantically tap dancing
until the fever is gone.

I found out moons ago
there is no sleep for poets at 3:00 AM
when only stars and inebriated friends sharing taxis
can be found, stumbling,

like I am with these words.

In the Corner at Starbucks

Get through the pleasantries;
small talk at Starbucks
over pumpkin spice lattes
introductions: singer to artist,
artist to headliner
at a comedy club,

and then, there is me

sitting in the corner
penning this poem on a napkin;
this woman
who can't really call herself a poet,
yet.

What will it take to make it real;
one more book, two,
a book signing
(with more than five people)
clamoring for an autographed copy,

or can I just feel it in my soul
deep down
where the pounding won't stop
until keys click out thoughts
that stick in your throat
burn you, from the inside
to get out;

this ache I've had all my life;
nagging noise
of a mesmerizing muse
begging to be heard-
dying to be proclaimed

a poet.

Tangled Versions of Us

These little things like sighs;
like brush of fingertips across waiting skin
send soft breaths to petaled places
where thirst for love feels more innocent
than any blossoming flower we have held.

Lips do more than whisper and when
sweet nothings leave prints
and giggles find a place in awakening thoughts.
We meet in meter keeping perfect time
in intimate increments.

Keep my bare feet on a blooming path
and my hands longing for yours

and stay close enough to touch the tremble
when rains come and feel every tousled strand
as we sway

into tangled versions of us.

Softening the Lines

Bring me flowers,
to wear, now
on skipping, laughter in my hair
days. You always give me pink
for symmetry
and the sweetness of you

with me.

Kiss my lips while they are warm
inviting melt,
pulsating, petal silk skin;
your hands, turning winter
into spring.

These autumn days swirl past
with cold looming, sweet
but never fearful
with your fingers softening lines,

tracing life,

reviving breaths
even after I take my last.

Blues and an Overflowing Tip Jar

Walking past windows-
a fogged up and dusty portrait
of some white shirt, black tie event;
smoke swirling someone's life story
from a Steinway piano, each note
another semblance to drink to.
A lady at the corner table,
all too familiar with his gaze
as memories roll down cheeks,
she mumbles under her breath,
"What a waste of good lipstick."

Scenes play out quietly
from behind stained glass;
embroidered hankies lending calm
to stirred up cocktail of dreams
in watered down versions
of he said, she said ramblings
under subtle Friday night moons
with old demons, making new friends.

This rain, this rain drowning pasts-
feet shuffling through puddles
kicking bruised egos to the curb,
slinging blame like leftovers
to anyone who will listen.
Minds can be small, hearts smaller
as battered souls keep searching,
searching, for a soft place to land

Strands of Redemption

They say the meek shall prosper-
rise from ashes and shame.
Broken people whisper louder;
shine, under clandestine stars,
shimmering, making peace
from pieces of yesterday,
bartered and branded as shiny
new flowered tomorrows.

Oh, the pain, the pain of reality,
stark, glaring rays, almost blinding.
There you are, doubtful, resistant,
trusting of a resentful resemblance
of someone we used to know.

You stand there, judging me,
turning over the hour glass,
foot tapping, waiting for a response
to this trial without a jury
you have imposed; this unjust,
unrequited obsession.

I never would have thought
I would be standing here,
those pointing fingers, mocking;
birds leading me home,
away from scrutiny, ridicule.

These pearls, these pearls
pure as driven snow,
soft, never tainted by ugliness;
strands of redemption 'round my neck
like winged promise,
pronounced in calming syllables
until ache is quieted by clasped hands
and soothing reverberation.

Everything Shiny

I wondered why stars were my diamonds
and sun, my savior of soul.

When pain visits like monsters under the bed;
chest beating like so many nights
when the noise wouldn't stop,

I forget to breathe.

That is the 2:00 am ache
that never ceases to awaken me
even now, when covers are warm
and gentle arms
whisper nightmares away.

I see brides with Fathers on their arm
and smiling schoolgirls with dreaming eyes,
but *his* eyes are what make me cry.
They are proud, accepting
with a lifetime of love pouring
from two little ducts.

No girl should have to be without a Daddy.

She needs glitter, glimmer and everything shiny;
wildflowers picked and placed in her hand
so she can wake up knowing
she is loved.

I wondered what happened to that little smile,
those dreaming eyes;
why I never knew what it felt like
to make you proud just one time,

and now behind every syllable I write
each little accomplishment,
there is a secret wish

just to prove you wrong.

A Manuscript Missing Pages

I found a manuscript in the attic;
crumbling paper decomposing
into fragments of a life.
I saw a resemblance in this girl;
brown haired, pale faced,
quick paced, smiling energy
turning inward.

I read her words hoping to know
what became of this bashful, dreamy eyed
fatherless bud picking wildflowers;
this babies on her hip,
fingers intertwined,
one foot on the accelerator,
the other on the brakes
mess of nerves.

She spoke of love calmer than her stride,
whispered psalms sweeter than the roses missing
from her cheeks and in these pages,
there was life. There were fields, stars;
there were moons over river water

and satin soft comfort not seen in Polaroids
that she left; the only evidence
of a past filled with more shade
than any Southern girl would find
on any given Summer day

and there was sun.

If Not For Flowers

An engagement of vocabulary
rolling sweetly off of tongues;
syllables coupled in undertones,
gently timed like a ballerina's steps,
ethereal pieces sewn into cadence
sipped and soaked into every pore
of some poet's mere existence.

If not for flowers, where would we find art
flowing like tumbleweeds across barren plains
shaky adjectives reverberating from willows
into the very beat of a breaking heart
just aching for the revelation
of another perfect sunrise-
another misty eyed ocean to paint.

There is no time for sleeping
with trains to remind her of those last days
when he still had warm hands and dreams
of one more walk in the sand, dance of hair
on autumn nights when moons were full
and treetops were the highest thing he could see.
She smiled when one lone star fell;
fireflies circling for a collective whisper, *goodbye.*

By December

I.

In May
rain tiptoed out
as pretty peonies
blew about in the
after-rain. It was
only proper
that I should meet you
in my perfect season
when petals bloom
at first sight-
pink as the possibility
of love.

II.

July
was warm, this Texas sun
like my blush, born
of something heart melting.
We thought that summer
would never come and the cry
we worried about never fell;
as most perfect days go,

it shined. There were lilies
falling softly before the train,
Delicate words vowed
behind veiled whispers
only lovers could hear
and adhere to.

III.

By December,
feelings came
and never went
since you took my hand;
never softer than now
when perfect mornings
are the ones
beginning next to you.
Seasons change
like butterflies
in this metamorphosis,
but, my dreams never have.
Your laughter fills this room
and my face lights it up.
Flutters still happen here
when those brown eyes
meet with mine.

I Will Bring The Harp

Your tears
run down my face
and that sinking feeling you get
resonates;
my voice, shaking
in prayer.

Your laughter
fills empty, blue places
like a net to catch
my fall.

Let me;

let every flutter I feel
play in your hair,
find smiles in your sleep
and keep covers warm
until morning comes

and when sun hides
from pale faces
and stars no longer glimmer,

I will bring the harp
to golden places
and play an overture

if you hold the gate open
for me.

In the Rearview

She had learned not to make waves
hopscotching through life
never throwing the stone hard enough
to break through those thick walls

of discontent.

Years away,
there was a boy;
quick witted with a smile

that still melts moons.

and they would both be in
for the struggle.

His rage dissipated
into puddles of grace;
her tiny hands
turned to slender fingers,
still intertwined at 3AM

two sets of footprints seeking solace
at the end of winding roads

of fate,

wishing to stars
for golden rays
to peek through cracks.

It is easier to feel stronger
when the glass is half full.

Crackers in Bed

They weren't your nightmares
to chase away;
fears to calm,
and you never signed up to rescue me
from my own imagination.

Sometimes you have to save someone
More than once;
2:07 AM therapy sessions-

diagnosis: my past.

No one told me
that abuse come in many forms
and that by any definition,
control is not love.

Pain trickles slowly
like hydration from an i.v.
as life flows back in

through transfusions of love.

Wind Song

Under these stars, be still.
Listen to sounds of humming,
chords from winged wind song.
Bring peace to breezes, smiles
to strangers and lift your eyes
to see miracles in the making;
treasures that lie where only
kindness lives. Be humble,
under moonlight dreams, begging
light of new beginnings, swirling
in calmer breezes. Through flowers,
and sweet green meadows, laugh.
Hold hands with those in sorrow,
dance with joyful spirits, close
your eyes, fingers intertwined,
head bowed, and just be still.

Just Desserts

We could visit Paris, walk in the rain without an umbrella
and sit on the steps of Eglise Saint-Etienne-du-Mont
when the clock strikes twelve and we are back in that club
rubbing shoulders with Hemingway; shots of wisdom
swirling in cocktail glasses with cherries, olives
or whatever you fancy; culture parading its diversity
in paintings by Picasso that make you take a second look
and wonder where a mind could go to find such muse,
blue and clearer than sea water, these syllables
that taunt you in your sleep, weigh on you in vibrant colors
of indigo, azure; scents of lavender filling pretty stationary
tempting you to write, scratching you from the inside,
these words dying to escape from pink painted lips
that only want to feel that last goodnight kiss.

Lynda G. Bullerwell

About the Author

Lynda G. Bullerwell resides in Texas with her husband, Tim and her Autistic son, Junior. She is also the proud Mother of two daughters, and 3 beautiful grandchildren. Lynda has been writing poetry for over 30 years and considers it her passion and a release for emotions since she was a child. Lynda released a collection of poetry entitled "Into the Light" published on October 16, 2013 by Water Forest Press, and has been published in literary magazines including Hudson View, Skyline Review, Epiphany Magazine, Writefromwrong, Miracle e-zine and Struggle magazine.

www.ingramcontent.com/pod-product-compliance
Lightning Source LLC
Chambersburg PA
CBHW051817040426
42446CB00007B/710